UNSTUFF YOUR HOME

SIMPLE HOUSE CLEANING HACKS TO
DECLUTTER AND TIDY UP YOUR HOME, LET
GO OF UNUSED THINGS, ORGANIZE YOUR
ROOMS, AND ACHIEVE FREEDOM ONCE AND
FOR ALL

LILLY NOLAN

FREE GIFT!

Do you want a checklist that can help you tidy up your home in only one week?

In order to thank you for reading my book, I included a 7-day declutter checklist for you. This printable cheat sheet will help you clean your home room-by-room easily!

Get yours now >> https://dl.

bookfunnel.com/jbyr5w8qpf

contained within this document, including, but not limited to, errors, omissions, or inaccuracies.

INTRODUCTION

Everyone gathers possessions in one form or another. Depending on how you accumulate possessions in your life, it can create clutter in your home that may be significantly more than that of other individuals. Handling clutter can be a challenge if you don't know the right steps to take.

The clutter in your home may be in the form of clothes, shoes, toys, dinnerware sets, and so on. As you pile up these items without discarding, you slowly create clutter in your home.

Since you may struggle to deal with clutter in the home, I'm confident that this book will provide a solution to your problem. The answer it offers includes vital information on how to stop yourself from accumulating clutter and how to eliminate existing clutter in the home through decluttering.

Solutions such as learning to say no to gifts, decluttering public and private spaces in the home, and maintaining the habits you develop are all introduced. If you are in doubt about my ability to help you, then let me tell you a little about myself.

I am a 37-year old mother of two kids who used to be in a similar predicament. I was working for a magazine company and used to struggle with clutter before I eventually quit the job.

During my time at the company, there were days I had to take some of my work home, to meet deadlines. Despite this action, I was usually unable to do much at home. Why?

You guessed it; in great part, it was due to the presence of clutter in my home. This created distractions that made it difficult for me to focus on my work. I was working hard, but inefficiently. Books and magazines were stacked all around me. Laundry piled up. The flow of the furniture just didn't work. I couldn't really get anything done with all of the "junk" around me.

To overcome this problem, I started researching ways to get rid of clutter. Through my research, I learned a lot about decluttering. As the name implies, it is the process of getting rid of clutter.

After engaging in the decluttering process

around my home, I noticed changes in my life. It improved my concentration and efficiency while working. Also, I learned to be content. Through contentment, I was able to avoid falling into the trap of accumulation, which would have caused me to create more clutter.

By going through this book, you'll learn many things. When you apply the tips and information in this book, benefits accrue to you. Things you will learn include:

- Why you accumulate "stuff"
- Understanding hoarding, its effects, and symptoms
- Learning about minimalism and Danshari
- Applying Danshari to your life
- Unstuff your home
- Keeping up your new habits

As you learn about these areas and apply them to your life, you will quickly start noticing changes. Before that, you must understand that you need to put in the time and effort to make these changes. Decluttering, as a process, takes a lot of time to complete.

Regardless, it is a process that grants you small wins that pile up. This means that you get the opportunity to apply the decluttering process to a small section of your home, like your bedroom, and then compare it with other parts. This will give you the motivation you need to complete the process.

When you apply everything you learn in this book, an example of the change you experience is an increase in the amount of money available to you. This is because you no longer buy things you don't need.

Eliminating clutter in the home can also make it possible for you to live in a smaller, less expensive apartment or home. Let me explain. I've had the opportunity to work with other individuals to help get rid of their clutter problems. Some of these individuals are those who continuously hoard things. These individuals have also learned to overcome this problem and engage in the decluttering process. As a result, they were able to move from a large apartment to a smaller, more economical and efficient space.

I am confident that this book will change your life through the information it contains. The information herein is tailored to address the various issues relating to clutter. These include the causes and effects.

Dealing with clutter is one thing you must do swiftly. Delaying this action will only further complicate your situation as it leads to a drop in your productivity, and can also affect your relationship with others. If you're struggling with hoarding, then you have no time to waste. Hoarding harms both your health and your home environment. Most of us think of the extremes of hoarding, based on what we've seen on television, for example. But hoarding isn't necessarily harmful only under those extremes. Do you:

- Buy excessive food at the grocery store?
- Have duplicates of many items in your home?
- Feel uncomfortable purging yourself of unused items?
- Have a lot of piles around the house?

These are signs of a more minor habit of hoarding, and it can be a real burden when it comes to how you live your life, and how you can fulfill your potential. Excess stuff doesn't just clutter your home; it clutters your mind and heart.

If you want to overcome these issues, then you must start now. As I said, decluttering is a process that takes time. Therefore, you can't waste any more time dragging your feet.

Are you tired of the clutter in your home? Are you excited to take steps to change your life for good? Begin your journey now by flipping over to the first chapter.

WHY ARE THERE SO MANY THINGS IN YOUR HOME?

"Don't own so much clutter that you will be relieved to see your house catch fire."

— WENDELL BERRY

A significant problem many individuals face today is that they have too many things in their homes. Books, clothes, shoes, plates, phones, wires, toys, and many more items occupy space in the house and are often never used. These items are what create clutter in the home.

If you understand and accept that this is a fact, then how do you accumulate these items in your home? The answer to this question can be split into three categories. These are the most common reasons why you collect things in your home. Let's quickly explore these reasons.

Purchases Over the Years

Consumerism is a lifestyle that has a significant impact on how consumers behave in the world today. Certain things promote consumerism in the world today. I spent time at a friend's house recently, and there were piles of unsorted clothing from purchases months and years ago. I've seen other homes with two, three, four bottles of the same cleaning solution. So, if you're "collecting" stuff like this, it may be time to examine why.

The first is the possibility of engaging in the mass production of some items, which results in a lower cost of purchase to the consumer. This is an effect of the availability of cheap labor in various countries such as China.

The top-quality marketing strategies in use by various companies today also promotes consumerism. Today, companies choose to target the insecurities of their consumers in a bid to get them to buy products.

Are you a woman, for example, who is conscious of her post-pregnancy stomach? Then companies will choose to advertise waist trainers to help you feel good about your stomach.

These are just some of the strategies in place to encourage consumers to purchase unnecessary products. Combining these strategies with social media, there is very little you can do to avoid coming in contact with these marketing campaigns.

As you give in to these marketing strategies over the years, you steadily pile up possessions that create clutter in the home. Since you believe there will be a time when these items will be useful, you find it difficult to discard them.

Things You Inherited

Another form through which you can acquire a lot of things in your home is through inheritance. In most cases, you also end up with inherited clutter. You can inherit some of these items as a result of any of these:

- If a member of family or friend needs to move to a smaller house or nursing home
- If you lose a loved one, and inherit some of their belongings

In both cases, the items you receive often have a sentimental value that makes it difficult to discard them. A leftover item from an individual that becomes your property is an inheritance. When your grandparents or parents die, it's common for the family to receive their possessions.

A client of mine amassed a large collection of Hummel figurines from her grandmother. They were all over the home, in every nook and cranny she could find. I asked her about them. She said, "Oh, those? I don't even like them. But they were granny's." We talked about how she could safely store them in the garage, and keep out one or two for display as a reminder of her beloved grandmother.

Gifts

Gifts are another means through which you can pile many unnecessary things in your home. Everyone receives a gift now and then, but you may not fancy all the gifts you receive. Despite your dislike for the gift, you may find it difficult to discard the gift. Another friend of mine has a "collection" of sweaters from his mom. He hates all of them, but doesn't have the heart to tell her, or to get rid of them. This is not an uncommon situation.

This is because you don't want to hurt the feelings of the individual giving the gift. Besides, most of us try to avoid getting caught after discarding these gifts. As a result, you end up holding on to something you don't need for long periods.

This action of holding on to gifts might sometimes be due to our lack of understanding of the word gift. For instance, that understanding is also one of the reasons why you might be really uncomfortable saying 'no' to someone giving you a gift. Without saying no, you will continue to accumulate gifts that turn into clutter in your home.

Going by the dictionary definition, a gift is something you receive from another individual without any need for payment. What this implies is that a gift can only remain as one if you have no obligation to the giver. Accounting for their feelings or the fear of discarding is an obligation to the giver that you create.

These obligations make the item you receive stop being a gift. When you understand the meaning of a gift, it becomes easier to let go.

So, why do we collect clutter?

Let's now take a look at some of the reasons we accumulate this type of clutter in our lives. Sit with each of them to see if they resonate with you. Take your time when reading this section – let's get to the root cause of clutter in your life. I'm here to help.

$\cdot$ $\cdot$ $\cdot$

Low-Self Worth

When you take time to break down the strategies various manufacturers utilize in their marketing campaigns, you notice there is a lot of emphasis on making you feel worthless. This is how they get you to buy their products. Through these strategies, and the impact of society today, you adopt the belief that acquiring more possessions can help boost your self-worth.

When you associate more possessions to higher worth, you steadily begin to accumulate clutter in your home. Since you believe your wealth indicates your worth, you use it as a way to overcome your feelings of worthlessness. This is when buying makes you feel better about yourself.

Besides, if you're unable to identify your worth, then you will seek external validation. This will often lead to people-pleasing habits. Due to these habits, you become unable to say no to others.

This is when you start accepting gifts that have no place or use in your home. Souvenirs from friends or gifts from your mother-in-law all find a way into your home to create clutter.

Low self-worth also creates a fear of failure in your life. This fear of failure can also cause an increase in the possessions you have in your home. This is possible when you start worrying about your ability to engage in the act of decluttering successfully.

Despite understanding the benefits of the process, your inability to take the first step towards decluttering will be detrimental.

The Need to Hold on to the Past

There are specific memories you hold dear, and items you associate with these memories. This is common among various individuals. We find it difficult to discard certain things that remind us of our past.

As a parent, watching your kids grow up fast can be overwhelming. Sometimes, you want to remember the times when they were just babies. To recall these memories, you may choose to keep their bed or hold on to drawings from their childhood. These items can serve as triggers for these memories. As triggers, you leave them in your home as keepsakes. Some of these items may be to remind you of times when you were more popular or successful; to help you remember that you should still be proud of yourself.

. . .

Other Reasons

In addition to the reasons above, there are other reasons why you may struggle with clutter in your home. For some individuals, the task of decluttering can seem overwhelming. So, they choose to avoid it.

Struggles with a disorder or physical disability can also lead to a pile up of clutter. The hoarding disorder, which I will introduce in the next chapter, is a common issue. In this case, calling a professional can provide a considerable benefit.

Although you may be unwilling to admit it, you might also struggle with clutter due to your lack of proper time-management abilities. This is a skill you must learn, and you don't gain it at birth. Without developing adequate time management abilities, you can never get down to the decluttering process.

Although everyone struggles with one issue or the other, you can always overcome these issues. Now that you know the reasons you're struggling with clutter in your home, it's time to learn about how to deal with them.

The Takeaway

- Clutter is a problem many individuals face which often results from the consumerist lifestyle. Low self-worth often promotes the need to attach worth to the number of possessions you own.

- Memories of the past can prevent you from discarding some old items in the home. Clutter can also result from disorders such as hoarding.
- Many people without time-management skills and those that struggle with indecision are prone to have clutter in their houses.

2

CHANGE YOUR PERSPECTIVE ON HOARDING ITEMS

"Hoard food and it rots. Hoard money and you rot. Hoard power and the nation rots."

— CHUCK PALAHNIUK

What is Hoarding?

Hoarding is a compulsion that leads an individual to hold on to things. For an individual with a hoarding disorder, they will find it challenging to throw away or part with any of their possessions. The value of the item in question isn't a factor when it comes to hoarding.

Although many people may consider hoarding to

be harmless, it usually has harmful effects. These effects can include:

- Financial: spending excessively on consumer goods, paying for storage, living in a house much bigger than you need.
- Social: difficulty with friends and family members.
- Legal: creating environments where neighbors might complain, or city/municipality codes are being broken.
- Physical: unhealthy living conditions, clutter to an excess where physical space is compromised, unclean, and dangerous.
- Emotional: using physical objects to hold onto emotional difficulties.

These effects of hoarding will affect the hoarder and other individuals he/she interacts with, such as family and friends. You may ask yourself, what is the difference between a hoarder and a regular individual? This is a common question people ask.

To identify a hoarder, the quantity of items in their possession is the most useful factor. These items can occupy entire homes, and make it difficult for other individuals to move around the house. It creates clutter in areas like stairways, desks, countertops, and other surfaces in the home.

The items you can find in possession of a hoarder consist of the following:

- Magazines, newspapers and photographs
- Food items and household items
- Clothing, shoes, and accessories
- Plastic or paper bags and excessive boxes
- Excessive animals, and their "messes."

There are several levels of hoarding into which you can classify hoarders. These levels are known as the "Clutter Hoarding Scale," developed by the National Study Group on Compulsive Disorganization. They include the following:

1. Hoarding Level One: On this level, the clutter is not in excess. The home is still sanitary and safe since there is proper ventilation with no odors, while stairways and doors remain accessible.
2. Hoarding Level Two: Here, you notice garbage cans overflowing with trash

while light mildew becomes noticeable in the bathrooms and kitchen. You can find one exit in the home blocked, while there are two or more rooms filled with clutter. There are limited signs of proper housekeeping, light odors, and pet waste or dander puddles present.

3. Hoarding Level Three: The homes on this level have strong odors emanating from them, with noticeable clutter outdoors. Food preparation areas are heavily soiled, and there is an unusable bathroom or bedroom in the house. You may find too many pets in the home, and there is usually excessive dust.

4. Hoarding Level Four: Counters with rotting food, pet damage around the home, dangerous electrical wiring, sewer backup, flea infestation, and lice on the bedding in the house.

5. Hoarding Level Five: Clutter in the home renders the bathroom and kitchen unusable, utilities such as water and electricity will be disconnected, rodent infestation, and feces of animals and humans around the house.

From these levels, you can infer that level one is mild, while level five is severe. The level five hoarding will have a significant effect on your daily activities, while the impact of level one hoarding may be insignificant to a great extent.

The issue of hoarding may develop due to compulsion. In this case, compulsive buying, compulsive search, or compulsive acquisition. Compulsive search is noticeable in hoarders who are similar to collectors. These individuals are in search of items that they tag as being unique or perfect, despite these items as being normal to others.

Compulsive buying is identifiable in individuals that always make a purchase anytime they feel it is a bargain. The case of compulsive acquisition refers to individuals that are always looking to get anything that is free. These can be things as useless as flyers.

The presence of the hoarding disorder may be an indicator of another disorder, but in most cases, it is on its own. Other disorders that are indicated by the hoarding disorder include:

- Depression
- Obsessive-Compulsive Disorder (OCD)

- Obsessive-Compulsive Personality disorder (OCPD)
- Attention-deficit/hyperactivity disorder (ADHD)

Hoarding disorder may also be a sign of an eating disorder, although this may be rare. Other disorders associated with hoarding include:

- Prader-Willi syndrome (a genetic disorder resulting in obesity and intellectual disability)
- Dementia
- Pica (intake of non-food materials)
- Psychosis

Who is Likely to Experience it?

An individual with a hoarding disorder can be straightforward to identify. Most of these individuals usually gather a large number of items that create clutter in their homes and find it difficult to discard these items. You can also check for these symptoms:

- Piling up clutter in various rooms until they become unusable

- Gathering items for which there is no storage space or immediate need for
- A compulsion to keep things with a sudden change in mood anytime there is a thought of throwing out these items
- Difficulty engaging in organizing and planning
- Procrastination, avoidance, perfectionism, and indecisiveness
- Social isolation, financial challenges, loss of living space, health hazard, relationship discord
- Embarrassment and feeling overwhelmed by their possessions
- Going through their trash in case they threw out an item by accident
- Always suspicious of other people touching their possessions

Although there are certain similarities between hoarders and collectors, they aren't the same. For collectors, they are intentional in their search for items. They may seek out a specific item such as a model car, or stamps, categorize these items, and put them on display. Another noticeable difference is that collectors organize their things for the purposes of their collection.

Reasons People Hoard

There are different reasons why people hoard items. The following are some reasons to help you understand yourself and other individuals that hoard:

1. You strongly believe that an **item will be of value or use in the future**. These are the items you think you will use later, such as excesses from your last house renovation project or things you think you can sell for a high price in the future, such as collectibles.

2. Your **inability to recall where you stored certain items** in the home can lead to hoarding. When the need for such a thing arises, you buy another on impulse to meet your pressing need. As a result, you have multiple items performing the same function.

3. The idea that an item has **sentimental value** will impulsively make you hoard the item. These items can be photos, books, clothes, and more. Sentimental items are those to which you attach specific memories and emotions.

4. **When you think an item is irreplaceable and unique**, discarding it becomes very difficult. A sweater knitted by your grandmother, something you received from someone who has passed away, and things that are no longer in production.

5. Depending on the price you got an item, **you may consider it to be a bargain**. This will promote the assumption that you may never be able to get it at such a price in the future. To avoid the possibility of paying more for an item later, you will choose to hold on to it, rather than throw it away.

6. **Indecision** is another reason why you may be hoarding an item. Is it essential or not? When you have a challenge answering this question, you may opt to hold on to the item.

7. You may attach certain events, individuals, and memories in your life to some items in the home. These items assist in jogging your memory about these events or individuals. The belief that **only these items can promote**

vivid recollection will lead to hoarding.

Effects of Hoarding

Hoarding is an action that has an impact on you both physically and mentally. The implications of hoarding are noticeable in your environment and your behaviors. In this section, we will focus on various areas in which you can be affected.

Physical Impacts

Hoarding is an action that creates unhealthy living conditions for you. As a hoarder, it will be a challenge to engage in basic daily activities. These include actions like cooking, bathing, and cleaning.

Your inability to perform these actions will affect your hygiene, while your access to a proper diet will be impossible. These lower the effectiveness of your immune system and expose you to illnesses.

When you hoard things, food containers will pile up in the home, and spoiled food will also promote the growth of fungus and mildew. Along with the poor air circulation, you will become a victim of mold problems.

Mold problems can aggravate any existing health

problems, trigger your allergies, and also cause damage in your respiratory system.

Pest infestation is another problem you face due to hoarding. With items decomposing in one hidden corner or the other, they become attractive to pests such as rats, ants, flies, cockroaches, and so on.

Since these pests know how to remain hidden, it will be challenging to get them out of the home. This is how the severity of your pest infestation increases over time.

Other Impacts

Hoarding usually affects you mentally. This is identifiable in your struggle with depression, anger, and resentment. These are often an effect of traumatic or stressful events in your life.

It is also common for hoarders to exhibit social withdrawal. This is because they will usually choose their possessions over their friendships or relationships with others. This can lead to conflict between the hoarder and other individuals.

If you're a hoarder living in a rented apartment with neighbors, you may have been in numerous legal disputes due to your living habits. Neighbors complain about the pests, dirt, and smell that generate from your home. Don't assume the world is against you, but see this as a push for you to make a change.

Hoarders also go through financial difficulties that never seem to go away. This is an outcome of their inability to separate valuable items from those that are worthless. Your purchases as a hoarder are to get something new to grow your collection. Also, you may find yourself having challenges keeping a job or even getting one.

Your safety is also at risk as a hoarder. This is because you may be living in buildings with structural damage or using appliances that are damaged. Since you find it difficult to let a professional come into your home and take a look, you choose to leave things as they are.

It would help if you understood that faulty electronics, stoves, and other appliances have a high risk of resulting in a fire. Once a fire starts, it will quickly spread to other areas of the home since your collection will consist of highly flammable objects.

The Takeaway

- Hoarding is a disorder in which an individual is compelled to hold on to things.

- Hoarding can affect you financially, emotionally, legally, socially, and physically.
- Compulsive buying, compulsive search, and compulsive acquisitions are different compulsions that result in hoarding
- The symptoms of hoarding may indicate depression, obsessive-compulsive disorder (OCD), obsessive-compulsive personality disorder (OCPD), and attention-deficit-hyperactivity disorder (ADHD). It can also indicate psychosis, dementia, pica, and Prader Willi syndrome.
- Hoarding is noticeable in individuals of all ages and becomes more severe the older an individual gets.
- Hoarders may be exposed to dangers such as structural damage, pest infestation, stress, depression, and more.

3

MINIMALISM AND DANSHARI

"The first step in crafting the life you want
is to get rid of everything you don't."

— JOSHUA BECKER

What is Danshari?

Decluttering is an art, some would argue. It's
not as simple as throwing things away, or not
collecting things in the first place. The mantra, "less
is more," applies when decluttering, and Danshari is
a way to wrap your mind and heart about the decluttering process.

Many of us are more familiar with this concept

through two prominent Japanese minimalists; Fume Sasaki, who lives in a tiny house with only 150 "possessions," and Marie Kondo, the recent Netflix star and purveyor of keeping things that "spark joy." But, Danshari is much more than these two individuals.

In many ways, Danshari is inspired by the Shinto religion, which focuses on the energy of all things around us. Shinto, in this context, is about "treasuring what you have; treating the objects you own a disposable, but valuable, no matter their actual monetary worth; and creating displays so you can value each individual object are all essentially Shinto ways of living." (Dilloway, 2019)

In its simplest form, Danshari consists of three Japanese Kanji (or symbols) which mean:

- Refuse (Dan)
- Throw away (Sha)
- Separate (Ri)

Dan – To Refuse

To refuse means you should limit the flow of items into your home and life. You have to be excellent at this job to reduce the clutter in your life. There are various actions to take if you want to refuse. Now, this might seem difficult, and at first it is. But, when we give our friends and family members other options, it can make everyone feel at ease.

For example, you can start by distributing a gift exemption certificate. By sending this certificate, you can let your friends and family know that rather than exchanging gifts, you will prefer other ways for both parties to relish the season.

You can also take other actions, such as:

- Asking for good deeds such as car washing, snow shoveling, etc. in place of gifts
- Propose a donation to your favorite charity, or a charity of their choice
- Bring up the idea of a gift-free holiday like doing kind things for each other
- Letting them know that time spent together is the best gift of all

These are just a few, and there are many other actions you can take to avoid gifts.

Another step to take in refusal is to avoid collecting freebies. Samples and trials are popular things that just create clutter in your home. These can be in the form of calendars, pens, notebooks, or magnets, all with a company name. Being polite is one of the reasons why you often collect these freebies, but you can also learn to decline politely.

Choosing minimalism is another way to achieve refusal. It helps you reduce your consumption to only your needs.

Sha – To Throw Away

This is another step that helps simplify your life. This is a crucial part of the decluttering process in which you discard unnecessary items in your home. There are some simple actions you can take to apply this in your life effectively.

You can start by adopting the idea of discarding one item a day. This is a much simpler and faster way to engage in decluttering. The item you choose to discard can be anything in the home. As long as you're not bringing any new item in, you will see noticeable changes in the house.

Some items that you feel can still be useful should go into a donation box that you can store in your garage. This is to make it easier to move when it is time to donate.

It can really clear your mind, heart and spirit to "let go" of things that you're holding onto – with love. For example, you can give heirlooms to other members of your extended family or donate them to a charitable organization. You can also take a photo of something that is very special to you before you let it go; sometimes that makes it easier. I also recommend selling them yourself, and then donating the money or using it for something essential to you.

If you're holding on to an item of historical value, then you can boost the inventory of a university or museum around you. For collections, you can save just a piece or two for yourself. A friend of mine recently moved overseas, and had to leave most of her book collection in the United States. She chose ten of her favorite books to bring with her. You can go through a similar exercise with any collectibles - save your absolute favorites, and limit them to a low number, donating or selling the rest.

The best option is usually to avoid collecting these heirlooms in the first place. As you do this, also remember the things in your wardrobe and kitchen.

- Clothes that don't fit
- Appliances and pans you don't use
- Clothes you don't wear
- Shoes and purses you don't wear or use more than a few times a year

All these and other items you find should leave the home. Go through your storage rooms and other places in your home and bring out all the things you don't need. Donate things to local charities, or places where they can use items. For example, in my town, there are domestic violence and homeless shelters that are always appreciative of items that can go to help those in need.

Ri – To Separate

This is the last part, and it involves eliminating any form of attachment you have with any possessions in your home. Learning to do this is simple, and there are some tips to help.

The first tip is to learn to appreciate your space. You should understand that not only does possession create clutter, but clutter also occupies your space. Understanding that space creates room for creativity can be of help.

With clutter around, you're only going to struggle with discord and chaos. To engage in the process of separation, you need to start anew. In the process of decluttering, this involves bringing out everything you own and then letting in only those that you're sure you cherish and need.

For instance, you can choose to discard your

current schedule and create a new one. On this new schedule, you make sure you slot in only activities that add to your life in one way or the other.

In the case of your possessions, keep only the essential items, and be sure they are in their appropriate storage locations. Nothing should be on your countertops, and make use of drawers and cabinets.

You must understand that the concept of Danshari also encompasses your mental clutter in addition to physical clutter.

Less is More – Danshari Mantra

The concept of "less is more" is the focal of how we can think and feel when decluttering our lives, using the methods discussed in this book. In life, we tend to get caught up in excesses, for many reasons. The discipline that can be developed by thinking, seeing and feeling that "less is more," can be quite freeing. This concept is noticeable in both Danshari and Wabi-Sabi.

Many advocates of the Danshari minimalist lifestyle included Steve Jobs, Marie Kondo (who we've mentioned), and Buddhist or Zen monks.

Another important concept that relates to Danshari is "Wabi-Sabi." This is a Japanese concept that also promotes the idea that less is more. "Wabi" can mean an "understated elegance," while "Sabi" means "accepting imperfections with pleasure."

This concept accepts three things in life. These are:

- Nothing is perfect
- Nothing is finished
- Nothing lasts

Through an understanding of Wabi-Sabi, you can appreciate things the way they are, rather than focusing on how they should be. The acceptance of imperfection is in contrast to the constant pursuit of perfection, which is prevalent all around us.

This is the pursuit of relationships, achievements, and possessions. In the end, all you end up with is depression, stress, hasty judgment, and anxiety.

Why Should You Accept it?

As we've discussed, the notion of decluttering is not just about "stuff" in your home, car or workspace. The "stuff" we collect often goes much deeper than that. So, the notion of "less is more," can help clear our hearts, minds and spirits...as well as our home of needless clutter.

Let's take a look at a few reasons to explore how this mindset can benefit you.

It Grants Emotional Relief

In life, various things lead to emotional turmoil. One of the most common is when you lose your possessions. This can be due to a fire outbreak or a natural disaster.

The concept of less is more promotes the idea of having less emotional attachment to your possessions and other aspects of life. As a result, you're less likely to experience an emotional breakdown in the event of any loss of property. Although it may be going too far, some individuals also apply this concept to their relationship with others.

This is a means through which you can avoid being under the control of past events or emotions.

It Promotes Backpacking

As we discussed in the previous chapter, a severe issue that leads to clutter is hoarding. The opposite of hoarding is backpacking. This is one thing you adopt when you learn that less is more.

The lifestyle of a backpacker involves traveling around the world without anything but a backpack. The items in this backpack are all the possessions you own. As a backpacker, you value memories and experiences over the accumulation of possessions.

The fewer possessions you own, the better your mobility.

It Promotes Decluttering

This should be a no-brainer. When you accept to live with less, you begin to discard your excesses. You may not recognize that you're a hoarder, but if you have things around the home that you never use, then you're one.

You Control Your Words

The idea of less is more also extends to your words. When you talk too much, you run the risk of getting into trouble. You may even end up exposing things you shouldn't.

In your relationship with others, learning that less is more can prevent you from causing conflict. You learn to say only the things you need to. A few words can help you get your point across without things escalating into a full-blown argument.

The Takeaway

- Danshari is a Japanese word that translates to decluttering. It is made up of three Japanese kanji. You can split the word Danshari into Dan, Sha, and Ri.
- Dan means to refuse. It implies that you need to limit the flow of items into your home and life.
- Sha means to throw away. This means that you must be willing to discard all the unnecessary items in your possession.
- Ri means to separate. This means that you break off the attachment you have with your possessions as this hinders your ability to discard
- The Danshari mantra is "less is more."
- There are several reasons why you should accept this mantra including the emotional relief it grants. The mantra also promotes decluttering and the backpacking lifestyle.

4

HOW TO APPLY DANSHARI TO YOUR LIFE

"Instead of thinking I am losing something when I clear clutter, I dwell on what I might gain."

— LISA J. SHULTZ

There are times when you experience challenges and pressure in life. These situations can create both mental and physical clutter, depending on the extent to which they affect you. For many individuals, Danshari practice can provide an escape from these situations.

Most of the challenges and stress you go through are often a result of your lifestyle. When living a consumerist lifestyle, you're burdened with the need to acquire possessions. For many individuals, they end up deep in debt due to the need to live the consumerist lifestyle.

As you acquire more possessions, they occupy most of the living area in your home. The lack of space in your home hinders your creativity and productivity while creating stress in your life.

These are some of the issues you can solve through the danshari practice. Despite its effectiveness, you must submit yourself entirely to the practice. You will end up wasting your time and energy if you begin the process half-heartedly.

This can make you feel more frustrated, stressed, and confused than you were before. If you're ready to take action, let's move on to the next section.

How To Start Your Danshari Practice

The Danshari practice is crucial to your success in maintaining a clutter-free lifestyle. To start this practice, I will give you some steps you can take. Read on!

Commit to Your New Minimalist Lifestyle

The minimalist lifestyle is necessary for the Danshari practice. Since Danshari involves getting rid of clutter, you must be willing to live your life with whatever is left over after the decluttering process.

To commit to this new lifestyle, you must first understand your worth as an individual. When you learn your worth, you will break free of the common notion that your possessions indicate your worth. Assessing your real value and self-worth will make it possible to let go of the attachment you have to your belongings.

The minimalist lifestyle also involves learning to stop overcommitting. Go through your priorities again. Find out the areas creating issues in your life.

- Do you visit too many people?
- Are you always accepting requests from others?
- Are you committing to things that stray away from your priorities?

By assessing your life and actions, you can find out the areas where you spend most of your time and energy.

An inward look at yourself can also promote a shift towards the minimalist mindset. You can ask yourself these questions:

- Can I attain satisfaction without owning too many possessions?
- Am I happy with who I am?

To know we're happy with who we are, we must take away all the material possessions before assessing ourselves. This will give us the option to evaluate our true selves. This is not an easy path, but one that benefits us in a million different ways.

We must also assess the possibility of attaining satisfaction without having excess possessions. This is the moment when we learn to place value on experiences and relationships over possessions.

Looking inwardly, you get to know that all you are is a collection of your experiences and the memories you make. Through this understanding, you can understand that possessions add nothing to these experiences and memories. It is the people you spend your time with and how you spend your time.

Don't Focus on What You're Losing

If you choose to focus on what you're losing, you will never be able to let go of your possessions. To change your focus, you must change the way you think about Danshari. This is a concept that promotes the idea of being happy with who you are as an individual.

You must also understand that Danshari isn't just about living with fewer things. It helps you overcome the mindset in which you believe that your happiness depends on what you own.

A friend of mine recently moved from the central United States to Mexico. She was limited to one van of possessions she could bring with her, and that included her two dogs and a cat. She chose to bring only one suitcase of clothing, original artwork, one-of-a-kind furniture that she dismantled to fit, and utilitarian folding furniture that she could use when she arrived at her empty, non-furnished place in Mexico.

Instead of lamenting on what she had left behind, "I felt a freedom that I hadn't felt in decades. Paring down my belonging only to the bare essentials, what would fit in that van, was incredibly refreshing. And, I was doing it to start a new, exciting life."

Eliminate the Things You Don't Need

To fully adopt the Danshari practice, you need to start getting rid of the things you don't need. You can start from one item at a time, and then move on to full-scale decluttering.

Letting go of your possessions is difficult, so you

have to slide into it gently. Sometimes this process brings up tears, or laughter, or both. It's ok to feel those emotions as you go. If it becomes difficult, you can start with the most obvious clutter in your house. This can be old clothes or broken appliances. Things that don't bring up as many emotions.

What is most important is that you start now. This will give you enough time to develop and accept this new habit.

When you make a bold decision to go on with the full-scale decluttering process, you still need to be thoughtful in your actions. You must separate the necessary items from those that you no longer need.

For example, with your seasonal items, you should do away with things you time. Looking at items like Christmas decorations in September will have you thinking of the last time you used them, but by December, you're going to need them.

Decluttering can be an emotional process, depending on your approach. For individuals that choose to throw these items in the trash, it can be a considerable challenge. This is why you should always try other options first.

You can decide to hold a yard sale, donate to charity, or sell them online. If the thought of decluttering is an issue due to the money you spent on these items, then the opportunity to sell these items will make it less painful.

The Takeaway

- Danshari is a way to escape the stress and challenges you face in life.
- It minimizes stress through the clutter you eliminate, and you can overcome financial difficulties if you choose to sell and stop buying on impulse.
- To apply Danshari in your life, you must commit to minimalism.
- Committing to minimalism involves assessing the various actions you take in life.
- You must be willing to shift your focus from the things you lose to what you gain if you want to apply Danshari in your life successfully.
- Learning to let go of what you don't need is crucial in Danshari.

5

UNSTUFF YOUR ROOMS

"You don't have to face every skeleton in your closet before you can make some room in there!"

— CARMEN KLASSEN

Decluttering Is a State of Mind

Your new lifestyle of minimalism is dependent on your willingness to accept and engage in the decluttering process. It is a new state of mind that you must adopt. A state of mind in which you appreciate the space that you create by eliminating clutter.

To be successful in the process of decluttering,

you must go beyond saying, "I will declutter." Instead, you should start believing in the process of decluttering. This implies that you believe that the decluttering process will work for you, and help you develop a better life.

There are ways to help you develop this belief in the decluttering process. One of these is to think about the improvements you will experience in your quality of life. Creating a list of what you intend to achieve through the decluttering process is also very helpful. When you create this list, it is similar to writing out your goals. Having goals will motivate you to push forward when things get complicated.

Take out a piece of paper, and draw three columns with the following labels:

1. Decluttering will help me practically, by...
2. Decluttering will help me spiritually/emotionally, by...
3. Decluttering might be difficult for me, because...

Really sit with the exercise while you fill out those columns. Take your time, and understand where your emotions might be coming from. To have benefit beyond your immediate decluttering efforts, it's critical that you examine things a little deeper than you might have in the past. We all benefit when we look at ourselves this way, even if it's uncomfortable.

As I've talked about throughout this book, and the other related books that I've written on this topic, the decluttering process is a long-term experience. Many people find it easy to "give up" when they have to act for an extended period. But, try to avoid that trap. Keeping your goals in focus will enable you to stick with the long-term decluttering process.

Also, having a plan is necessary. Without a plan, you will keep running in circles without making any progress. Your plan is a guide to get you to your destination. The simple notes you take to identify how decluttering will help you, in all aspects of your life, can help keep you motivated and focused on the deeper reasons why decluttering can be so beneficial to you.

There is a sequential approach to completing the decluttering process and achieving the goals you set. Let's take a look at how you can declutter, room by room, area by area.

To unstuff your home, there are some actions you can take. You can think of these as the initial steps to ease the process of decluttering. These actions are applicable to all areas of the home.

Start by Eliminating Things You Don't Need or Want

You can fast-track the decluttering process by your actions during the initial stages. When going through your possessions, it is easy to identify the things you no longer need and those you don't want.

These are the items you should declutter first. Some things that fit this category include:

- Old clothes that do not fit, or that are worn-out
- Old magazines
- Old or broken appliances
- Old furniture
- Shoes that no longer fit
- Children's toys
- Sentimental items
- Gifts you don't want

There are many more items that fit into this category, and you will quickly identify them when going through your possessions. Toss them out as soon as you identify them.

You can have a box for those that will go into the trash can and another for those you will donate. This is an organizational trick that will save you any additional stress in the future.

Once you're able to separate these items, you're left with those you feel you need. You should understand that these items will still contain clutter. When organizing what's left, be sure to choose only the things that are essential to you.

This is an action that will help you cut down on the clutter in your home.

Clear All Surfaces

In every home, it is common to find different items taking up space on different surfaces. These surfaces include those in your living room, dining room, office, bedroom, kitchen, and so on. Although these may be essential items, you should consider them as clutter if they are not in their proper storage area.

The surfaces you should check during this process include the desk in your home office, kitchen countertops, sinks, dining table, ottoman, center table, and so on. Items that appear to be unnecessary should be moved off these surfaces.

Shred Old Letters and Recycle Junk Mail

Your old letters create paper clutter in your home. These can occupy space on a surface in the house or a drawer. Letters from a friend, a job applicant, those from service companies, your bank, and so on, all create paper clutter in the home.

Since paper is very light, you can have them flying around and littering the home as a result of wind. You can eliminate this form of clutter by shredding them. Shredding is a safer way of getting rid of paper clutter since it may contain some of your vital details. You don't want anyone going through your trash and finding out personal information.

If shredding isn't the right option, then you can choose to recycle junk mail. Various paper products, such as glossy paper can be recycled. Although you can recycle as it is, you can make an effort to remove the plastic windows on any envelope you want to recycle.

Be sure to keep the paper dry and remove your address labels before recycling. Things like paper labels and plastics (if it comes with your credit card) can contaminate paper recycling, so be sure to eliminate them.

Shredded paper often can't be recycled, so you must find a way to dispose of them properly.

Important papers can be filed away neatly. If the originals aren't needed, but you still want to keep the "paper," you can take a photo or scan the important document and keep a virtual file.

Discard Old Ornaments or Decorations

There are ornaments you may be hoarding in your home but never use. These will include those you bought during a family holiday one or two decades ago. Why do you still have them?

Many individuals will argue that these items serve as triggers for some of their important memories. This isn't a compelling argument. Take this time to try taking a photo of the item in question, does the picture trigger the same memory?

A few years ago, I went through a large box of photos and items that were sentimental to me. I wanted to get rid of the box, so I took the time to take pictures of things that meant something to me, and threw out the box. But within a week, my laptop was stolen. Everything that I had photographed was on that computer, and I had no backup. I was crushed, and lamented my loss.

Two months later, do you think I can remember what was lost? Do I remember the specific photos and items? No. But the memories are there, and I know that the experiences, even if never remembered, have shaped who I am today – so the memento doesn't mean as much as how things shaped my life.

I know it will, so there is no need to have the physical item around, and occupying your space. Your memories are stored in your brain, so without the item or not, you will still have these memories.

Throw Out Expired Products

Your freezer or fridge does an excellent job in helping you preserve your foodstuffs. Sometimes, maybe they do too much. Since you're sure of the effectiveness of these appliances, it is easy to keep items past their expiration.

At this moment, you must go through all the products in your freezer and fridge. Look for those that have been there for too long, and those that have expired. It would be best if you threw them out quickly to avoid consuming anything that can damage your health.

This check must go beyond your fridge or

freezer. Check your kitchen cabinets and other food storage areas. Canned food, spices, and other items beyond their expiry date should be discarded.

You can also separate those that are close to expiry. If you're sure you won't be able to use these items before the expiry date, then look for a way to give them out. You can ask friends and family or search for where they will be put to use. Wasting food isn't a great thing, so make sure to donate as much as you can and reduce your purchases to the essentials.

Use Vacuum Storage Bags

To save storage space, vacuum storage bags are excellent. Nonetheless, you must be cautious when using this form of storage. First, you must avoid sealing clothes for too long.

This is to avoid damage to the fabric due to the absence of air in the storage bag. For items that are special and delicate, such as a wedding dress, you should look for other storage options such as plastic containers.

To use the vacuum storage bags, you can choose to roll-up clothes instead of folding. This will help prevent the clothes from creasing while in storage.

Since the bags are fragile, look for a place to store

them away from sharp objects. This will prevent them from getting punctured and allow you to reuse them.

You can choose this storage option for some of your accessories, and out of season clothes. When these items are needed, you can break them out of storage.

The Takeaway

- Decluttering is a state of mind.
- There are several steps you can take to declutter the rooms in your home.
- Be sure to clear all surfaces and discard old magazines or documents.
- Old ornaments and expired products shouldn't have a place in your house.
- Use vacuum storage bags to save space in your closet.

6

PUBLIC LIVING SPACES

"Clear your stuff. Clear your mind."

— ERIC M. RIDDLE

Public spaces in the home are those areas where anyone can access without any restrictions. They include your living room, dining room, and kitchen. These are the areas we will be looking at in this chapter.

Kitchen

One of the few public spaces in your home that is a hub for clutter is your kitchen. Foodstuffs, plates,

cups, and appliances are some of the things respon-
sible for clutter in the kitchen. You can get rid of
clutter through these actions:

Clear Out Cupboards

Since cupboards are essential to storing items, it's
good to spend some time clearing out excess. Since
items in cupboards are "out of sight, out of mind," it's
common to pile them up with unnecessary things. In
clearing your cupboard, make sure you're getting rid
of duplicate or unused items.

Reduce the number of plates, pots, and cups in
the cupboards. For easy organization, limit the
number of plates and cups to just enough to get you
through a day or two. For a family, include a set for
each family member.

I recommend making it enough for a day, so you
have no option but to do your dishes on a daily basis.
Removing duplicates will increase the storage space
available for use. When arranging pots, put them all
in one cupboard.

You should invert the lids so there is the option of
stacking. Also, similar items should be stored
together. All plates should be in the same cupboard,
cups should be in a separate cupboard, and you can
have your cutlery sets in a drawer.

. . .

Rearrange Appliances

There are certain appliances that need to be in the kitchen. Some have to be on surfaces, while others should be in storage. Separate your appliances into categories, and organize them.

Your coffee maker and microwave are appliances that should have a place on the kitchen surface, for example, if you use them every day. Your food processor, blender, and electric grill are other useful appliances that can be in a storage compartment. You can easily get them out when you need them.

You may have appliances you don't use in the kitchen sitting on countertops. This is when you need to move these appliances to their appropriate storage locations.

Ingredients and Cereals

Go through your jars of herbs and spices first to find those that are expired, as we discussed previously. You don't want to make the mistake of feeding your family these ingredients. Throw them out to create more space.

Mason jars are excellent for the purpose of storing herbs, spices, and cereals. The transparency of these jars also makes it easy to know when you're running low.

For ingredients and other utensils you use only on special occasions, you can dedicate a drawer or cupboard for the storage of these types of items. This might be a drawer or nook you will open less often, so you must check the expiration date before using any item here.

Remember, your kitchen surfaces and counter-tops should be free of clutter. Anytime you return from grocery shopping, put each item in its proper storage location and not on countertops.

Living Room

Your living room is a place for your everyday use. It is the gathering room for every member of your family. You can choose to watch television, read a book, go through magazines, or just have a chat in the living room.

The versatility of the living room provides an opportunity for clutter to pile up. Here are some of the things that create clutter in the living room and how to deal with them.

Books

When relaxing in the living room, you can choose to read a book or magazine. Since you may not complete the book on the same day, you may decide to place it on the table in the living room. This is in preparation for the next time you read.

Following your action, other family members may end up placing books on the same table. Soon, you will have a cluttered table. You can also have stacks of magazines on the floor in the living room.

To curb this form of clutter, you can install a bookshelf in the living room. This can be a standing bookcase or wall bookcase.

Being Smart with Furniture

One option to minimize clutter in the living room is to increase your storage options. You can make the most of your furniture by searching for those that serve multiple purposes. An example is an ottoman.

Depending on the ottoman you purchase, you can get a surface to sit or place items along with internal storage space. This internal storage will be useful in storing remotes, magazines, and TV guides.

Buy Baskets and Bags

Baskets and bags are useful storage solutions you

can have in the living room. Do you have blankets, pillows and other throws lying about in your living room or elsewhere in our house? How do you store these items? After you declutter items you don't need or use, you can use baskets to store things like blankets, seasonal clothing, towels, etc.

Discarding CDs and DVDs

DVDs and CDs are items that create a challenge when you need to decide to keep or discard. You may choose to keep certain DVDs or CDs, but never play them again. In the meantime, they're creating clutter. They don't have any monetary value, generally. Plus, so much is now available online through streaming services, there's no need to have a physical copy.

This will create clutter in the home that can pile up over the years. Take time today to go through these items. Identify those you will never open or watch again, and discard or donate them.

Rearrange

Rearranging the furniture in your living room is one way to create space. This can also be a means through which you discover all the toys left behind by your kids. You can use a basket to store these toys when you find them.

The arrangement you choose for your living room is important. Go online and search various minimalist designs you can use in your home.

Dining Room

The size of your dining table determines the amount of space you have left in your dining room. One question you should ask yourself is if you actually need that size of the table.

- Are you eight in your family?
- Do you entertain guests often?

Answering these two questions is an excellent way to determine the dining table size you need. If you can get by with four seats, then change to a dining table for four. This creates more space and you have nothing to lose.

Develop New Habits

The next thing to do is to develop healthy cleaning habits. These are habits to help prevent pile up of clutter in your dining room, including clearing place-mats and coasters off the table after each meal.

This improves the appearance of your dining room and leaves it clutter-free. If your dining room contains drawers and cupboards, then use them effectively. Cans and bottles should be put away, and learn to leave your countertops clear.

Dining rooms provide a good space for families to bond. In my family, we use our dining room to engage in fun activities like playing board games, assembling jigsaw puzzles and more. We've spent hours putting together our annual Christmas holiday puzzle, and playing the game of "Life!" If you do the same, then you should understand the level of clutter these create.

Always remember to put them into storage as soon as you finish the activity for the day. You may need to think of an alternative when you're short on storage space. You can search for portable or travel versions of these board games to minimize the space they occupy. They are still fun to play, but smaller.

The Takeaway

- Public living spaces are accessible by any member of the family. These areas include your kitchen, living room, and dining room.

- To clear clutter in your kitchen, you need to clear out your cupboards. Rearrange the appliances in the kitchen, and move out those appliances that shouldn't be there.
- The living room accumulates clutter in the form of books, magazines, CDs, DVDs, and so on. Install a bookshelf to store books and magazines in your living room.
- Get baskets and bags for storage.
- To clear the clutter in your dining room, you can purchase a smaller dining table to save space.
- Develop new habits of keeping the house clean and decluttered.

7

PRIVATE LIVING SPACES

"You're the boss of clutter, not the other way around."

— MONIKA KRISTOFFERSON

P rivate spaces are places that are accessible only to select members of the family. These are places where you go when you need to recharge and rest.

Bedroom

The bedroom is a place of rest at the end of the day.

Creating clutter in your bedroom will have a negative effect on your health. The clutter in your bedroom encourages feelings of guilt.

You might even feel guilty because you assume you're avoiding the job of eliminating clutter. This guilt creates tension which can induce stress in your life. One of the effects of stress is trouble falling asleep. When we have clutter in our homes, it's a symptom of clutter in our minds. This can keep us awake at night; tossing and turning as thoughts and concerns keep us awake. This emotional clutter shows up in many ways, and insomnia is not uncommon when we're dealing with "clutter."

To avoid these issues, you must take steps to declutter your bedroom, and also avoid the pile up of clutter in the future. You can take these steps to minimize clutter in your bedroom.

Develop New Habits

The first action you must take in controlling clutter in your bedroom is to develop new habits. These habits include putting clothes away each night, and storing shoes properly.

Shoes and clothes are common items that create clutter in the bedroom. When you get home tired, you just want to take off your clothes and rest. At this moment, you're not interested in where your clothes land or where you pull off your shoes.

You can make it a habit to arrange these clothes and shoes before jumping on your bed. If you're going to take a short nap, then you can arrange these items properly when you wake up later in the day. The goal is to ensure there are no clothes or shoes scattered across the room before you go to bed.

Go Through Drawers and Wardrobes

These are storage spaces where you may find the most clutter in your bedroom. You must be ruthless if you want to discard unnecessary items in your wardrobe and drawers.

Clothes that you don't wear any longer, and those that don't fit should be discarded. If the clothes are in excellent condition, then you can donate them to people that will appreciate it more.

Store Out-of-Season Clothes Properly

These are clothes that may occupy crucial space in your wardrobe. Since they won't be used for a while, then you can have a special storage for these clothes. You can get a plastic storage container and fold these clothes in.

Once you have them in containers, then you can move these containers under your bed, or place them on the top of your wardrobe. When it's autumn, move your summer/spring outfits into storage.

Repeat the process based on the current season, and you will notice an improvement in your wardrobe.

Organize the Bags

Bags in your bedroom include paper bags, plastic bags, reusable shopping bags, and traveling bags. You can move the traveling bag to a storage room until the next time you need it.

For the shopping bags, plastic bags, and paper bags, you can find a larger bag to store them. Fold them neatly so they occupy less space and are well organized.

Get a Hamper for Dirty Clothes

The hamper will serve as a laundry basket in your room. Since dirty clothes create the most clutter in your bedroom, then having somewhere to put them saves you a lot of trouble.

It doesn't have to be a hamper. You can get any other basket for this purpose. Finding one that matches the decoration of your bedroom is the best action to take.

Declutter the Distractions

Distractions in your bedroom usually come from the various devices in your bedroom. Consider getting ridding rid of, and banning anything with a screen from your bedroom. Smartphones, TV, and computers are some of the devices you might want to exclude. Take your bedroom from "digital" to "analog" to reduce these distracting devices.

Get yourself a classic alarm clock and read a book when on your bed. Limit your computer use to your home office, and charge your smartphone outside. While television may seem like a good idea for your bedroom, it is part of the reason you may struggle to fall asleep at night.

Get Rid of Containers

When you use makeup and moisturizers, you may end up having multiple half-used bottles on your dresser. These containers create clutter in your bedroom. Throwing them out is your next step.

To get to the point when you can throw them out, you have to use the contents of these containers. If there is any container you're sure you won't use, then find someone to give it to, or discard it.

Store Accessories in Bowls and Trays

Having a place to store your accessories is necessary to reduce clutter. You can create a storage space using a bowl or a tray. When you take off these accessories, simply place them into the bowl or on the tray.

Glasses, loose change, and keys are some things you can store in a tray. Jewelry like earrings and watches fit better in a bowl.

Bathroom

Your bathroom can get messy quickly if you don't make an effort to control clutter. Although it may be the smallest room in your home, it is used by everyone in the home. There are different items you pile up in the bathroom, and you need to start getting rid of them now.

The following actions will help you declutter your bathroom in a short time:

. . .

Leave Only Daily Use Products

To minimize clutter in your bathroom, make sure only the products you need daily are stored. These products include toothpaste, toothbrush, shampoo, soap, and so on.

Install a Hanging Shelf

Hanging shelves offer an excellent solution to your storage problem. This is because you can install them in places that would otherwise be impossible to use. For example, you can try installing a hanging shelf above your bathroom door.

You can use this shelf when you need to store extra products. These include shampoos, toilet paper, soaps, and other supplies.

Control Cord Clutter

There are certain appliances you need in your bathroom. Your curling iron and hair dryer are just a few of these appliances. The cords on these appliances can create clutter in your bathroom.

To control this clutter, you can start by searching for cordless appliances. If these are unavailable, then get a basket to store these appliances. All you need is a small-sized basket where you can place these appliances, before storing them out of sight.

I recommend using a magazine rack or file organizer for this purpose. You can attach these to the inside of a cabinet door or the side of the sink. This will help save the space under your sink.

Throw Out Expired Products

If you have a medicine cabinet in your bathroom, then this is the right time to go through the items in this cabinet. Check the expiration date on each product, and discard it when necessary.

In addition to medicine, you should also go through your makeup drawers. Throw out anything that is past expiration. When trying to organize these items back into their storage spaces, you can make use of dividers to separate the drawers. This will reduce the stress you go through when searching for items.

Separate and Combine Cleaning Products and Personal Hygiene Products

This is an organizational tip that is also geared towards your safety, since you want to make sure you keep any toxic cleaning products away from children or pets. But, beyond that, by organizing these items separately, you'll find that overall clutter is reduced. Especially when you combine duplicate bottles of glass cleaner, like I found at a client's home. Between the bottles under the bathroom sinks, kitchen sinks, and in the pantry – 7 bottles were combined to just one.

Same with personal hygiene products. Two partially used bottles of body lotion were combined to one, three same-brand shampoo bottles into one, and four bottles of same-brand liquid soap were integrated into two.

The Takeaway

- Your private spaces can serve as getaway areas when you need to be alone, rest, and recharge. The bedroom and bathroom are the two main private areas.
- Your bedroom is one place where you create a lot of clutter, and the clutter here also has a significant impact on you.
- Remove all distractions like TVs, laptops, and phones from the bedroom.

- When decluttering your bathroom, make sure you clear out expired products.
- Utilize bathroom space efficiently by introducing hanging shelves.
- Separate your cleaning products from personal hygiene products for safety

8

STORAGE SPACES

"If someone doesn't live with you, neither should their stuff."

— MONIKA KRISTOFFERSON

Storage spaces in your home include your garage, shed, and loft spaces or attic. For most individuals, these areas serve as the best places to dump things that may be useful in the future. Some of these items do turn out useful, but most don't.

Regardless of what may happen in the future, you can take steps to organize and declutter your storage spaces today. There are different actions you can take to achieve the results you desire.

The actions I discuss in this chapter are applicable to all storage spaces in the home.

Clear Out the Space

To perform a thorough job when decluttering and organizing storage spaces, your first step must be to take everything out. Depending on the items in storage, this may be a challenge.

If you have items that will be too difficult to move on your own, then get someone to assist you. Don't try moving heavy objects alone. You may end up hurting yourself in the process.

Discard Duplicates

There are certain items you use on rare occasions. Due to the frequency of their use, you may forget where you store them. The next time you need them, you often have to get another piece.

When you come across duplicates of an item, then you must discard the excesses. You can donate these items, or sell it to someone who needs it.

Store Similar Items Together

Storage spaces like your garage and sheds are

often used in storing gardening tools, sporting equipment, technical tools, hardware, and so on. When organizing these storage spaces, put these items together.

If you're storing them in containers, arrange the containers together. This will ease the process of finding your tools when you need them.

Use Labels

Labeling boxes and storage containers is a time-saving trick to apply during the decluttering process. With labels, you can easily find what you need anytime you head to your storage space.

Install Shelves

To efficiently use the space in your garage or shed, then you need to introduce shelves. Shelving is a way to utilize the surfaces above the ground.

There are shelves useful for storing sporting equipment, gear, and accessories. There are different designs depending on what you intend to store. You can find shelves for your soccer balls, in-line skates, basketballs, skis, and so on.

If you enjoy DIY projects, then don't shy away from creating storage shelves on your own.

Install Hooks, Racks and Clips

In addition to shelves, you can also use hooks and clips to store some items off the ground. Bicycles and gardening tools are some things you can store on these hooks and clips.

Bicycles can also be stored on sturdy racks if you prefer these to clips. You can get these at accessory stores around you. There should be wall studs into which you can fasten the racks.

Separate Your Space into Zones

Creating zones in your garage, shed, or loft will make things a lot easier. In your garage, you can have a separate zone for power tools, another for sporting equipment and protective gear, and another for gardening tools.

It is vital you store the protective gear near sporting equipment since they are usually used together. You can assign this zone close to where you park your car, along with the zone for camping gear.

This is to ease the process of loading and unloading these items into your vehicle.

. . .

Use Jars for Sharp Objects

Since you may find yourself performing some DIY projects in your garage or shed, there will be loose screws and nails lying around. These are hazards that can cause injury to anyone living in the house.

You can use jars to keep these objects secure. These jars can be arranged on the shelves in the storage space, and can come in handy during your next project.

Choose Storage Containers Wisely

The storage containers you use in your storage units can create clutter. If you have a mix of boxes, plastic containers, and other storage options, then you will have difficulties arranging or stacking them. You can choose to either use plastic containers or boxes when storing your possessions.

I recommend the use of plastic storage containers since they last longer and can easily be stacked. This will help save space in your home.

Dismantle Your Furniture

Before moving furniture into storage spaces, it is a good idea to dismantle the furniture. If you're moving an old desk, bed, dining set, or bookshelf, this is an important space saving-tip to adopt.

This will help you store items in a flat position while freeing up more space. Also, you can avoid trying to fill up the awkward spaces left from storing furniture in their assembled form.

Dealing with Pending Projects

DIY projects are fun activities, but also time consuming. Due to the time you need to spend on a project, it is common for projects to extend over a few days, months, or years. These pending projects usually occupy space in your garage or shed. One of my friends has a two-car garage full of projects. Some are beautiful pieces of furniture, waiting to be refinished. Once, when we went shopping together, he wanted to buy a "cool" dresser he saw. Now, I knew there was one in his garage, waiting and lonely. We laughed as I said, "Now, how is your old dresser going to feel about this new, young model being brought home."

If you find old projects you started a few years back, now is the time to ask yourself a few questions.

- Will I ever continue this project?
- Will it remain unfinished forever?

- Is this something that I can realistically finish?
- Is this project taking up valuable space, and creating stress instead of joy?

When you give honest answers to these questions, then you can make the right decision – to discard or keep. If you don't have a timeframe during which you expect to complete the project, then it may remain unfinished.

Unstuff Your Attic/Loft

In comparison to your shed and garage, the items in your attic may often be unique. Often, we keep things stored in these areas that are considered important, or are seasonal - in other words, we bring out the holiday decorations just once a year, and in between we put them in the attic. Garages and other storage areas like this are often, also, places where we put things when we're moving to our new place – but, years later the boxes remain unopened.

In this section, I will introduce you to some of the things you may find in your attic, that may need to move out.

.   .   .

Old Paperwork

These can be from your work, business, bills, or children's schoolwork. They include old letters, booklets, school reports, and more. Considering how difficult it is to handle paperwork just coming into the home, the challenge doubles when you have to go through old paperwork.

Another issue with storing paperwork in your attic is due to the dust and damp present in this room. Since paper won't survive under such conditions, you may lose the information on it. As we've mentioned, you might want to instead take photographs or scan the important information to keep it truly safe.

Hand-Me-Downs

The attic is the best place to store bags of hand-me-downs. These items quickly pile up in your home if people know you accept them. Although they're unwanted, they assume you need them in your home.

Unless they're actually useful to you, then you shouldn't be accepting hand-me-downs from anyone. You may be looking to get a toy or piece of clothing that will be useful to your child in a few years. This simple action is how you pile up clutter and create a mess in your attic.

You can also make an effort to donate these items to charity if you're having difficulties getting people to stop sending these items.

Photographs and Memory Boxes

Everyone likes to look at old pictures now and then, but storing them in your attic isn't the best option. Similar to the case of paperwork, these can get damaged due to the conditions of this storage space.

Since photographs are often sentimental items, you must learn to discard them if you intend to free up space in your home. You can start by creating soft/electronic copies of these photographs to ease the process, as we've mentioned before.

You may decide to keep a few items in these memory boxes, but you must be thorough in your selection. You can put these items on display if you feel they are that precious. Other items in memory boxes should be discarded to create more room.

Old Electronics and Appliances

We all enjoy a little bit of nostalgia. This is why we often hold on to our VHS machine or old cassette player. The problem is that you may never find any use for these gadgets in your home. DVDs, CDs, and online streaming make things a lot easier.

If you're piling up out of date electrical appliances in your attic, then you must take steps to discard them. You can find recycling centers to send these gadgets, or make extra cash by selling these items if they have any value.

The Takeaway

- Storage spaces in the home include your garage, loft/attic, and shed. Like every other space in the house, first, clear out these spaces when you decide to declutter.
- Look for duplicate items in storage spaces to discard and store like items such as tools together. Label boxes and containers in storage spaces to make things easier to find and create zones.
- Install shelves, hooks, racks, and clips for more storage and to maximize your space. Store sharp objects such as nails and screws in jars to prevent injuries.
- Dismantle furniture to make them easy

to store and reduce the space they occupy.

- Discard the hand-me-downs and old paperwork in your attic; throw out old appliances.

9

MAINTAIN YOUR NEW GOOD HABITS

"Change might not be fast and it isn't always easy. But with time and effort, almost any habit can be reshaped."

— CHARLES DUHIGG

The decluttering process is one that doesn't end. You have to keep decluttering at regular intervals if you want to maintain a clutter-free home. Nonetheless, the habits you develop also have a role to play.

You must do your best to avoid going back to your old habits. So, what can you do to avoid your old habits?

Question Your Actions

The easiest way to go back to old habits is to fall for temptations. When you switch to the minimalist lifestyle, everything around you suddenly seems more appealing. The new store down the street, the beautiful watch you see on Amazon, and so on.

Marketers and advertisers will also seem like they're working extra hard. Well, they are if we're honest. These marketing and advertising companies invest large sums of money to get the right information on customer behavior.

They know how to stimulate you and influence your purchasing decision. That is how they sell their products. Since they're doing their job so well, then you must do yours. Your job is to decide if the product is useful to you or not.

You can do this by asking yourself these questions:

- Can you survive without the product?
- Does purchasing this product stray away from the minimalist path you have chosen?
- Will you experience any improvements in your life?
- Will purchasing the product have a

noticeable impact on your finances?

These are some crucial questions you must ask yourself if you want to avoid falling for temptations. Answering these questions will help curb your impulse spending and help you maintain your stance on purchases.

Be Content

To ignore the temptations around you, learning to be content is vital. By being content, you can learn to silence the voices of marketers and advertisers desperate to get your money.

Knowing that you need to be content is the right step, but how can you achieve it? There are several ways to do this, and some may work for you, and some may not. You must discover what works for you. Here are some of the things you can do:

- Learn the act of gratitude
- Look inwards for the things about yourself that make you happy
- Identify little things that give you joy

Things you can be content about include your health, relationships, self-image, and so on.

Find Hobbies

Developing new hobbies, or engaging in previous hobbies is an excellent way to overcome your temptation and learn to be content. There are several hobbies you can try out.

The first is writing. Pick a book and pen, then start writing. Journaling is the most effective form of writing you can engage in at this point, and there are different types. Gratitude journaling stands out the most.

This is a form of journaling in which you write out things you're grateful for. Through this process, you can improve your happiness. Writing by hand eliminates the need to type on your smartphone and is more fun than you think.

Reading is another hobby you can engage in. You can read newspapers, books, or magazines. The internet and platforms like Kindle offer a means to access books and read news online. Another great benefit of reading is the opportunity to develop your brain and exercise your mind.

Some newspapers or magazines provide brain games like 'sudoku' and crossword puzzles. Don't miss out on these opportunities for self-improvement.

If you have an interest in music, now is the time to show off your skills with an instrument. Rather than watching music videos, you can bring your family together and give them a performance. This will also help in improving your family bond.

For those that are still learning to play instruments, you can opt to go to a live concert. Seeing your favorite musician or band live has a lot more impact than watching them through your smartphone.

Another excellent option is to express yourself through painting. Nothing feels better than splashing a few colors to create a masterpiece. No smartphone app can give you the same feeling you get from using a canvas to help ease your anxieties and stress.

Go for a Feature Phone or Install Ad Blockers

Smartphones are the products of advancements in technology over the years. These advancements are some of the reasons why it is easy to fall for the temptation of advertisers.

One way you can curb this temptation is to go back in time. To do this, all you need to do is purchase a standard feature phone. These are the phones that have fewer features than the conventional smartphone.

You can also call these devices 'dumbphones.' Most of them have standard features like text messaging, making and receiving calls, and internet access.

These phones usually come with low storage capacity, lower processing capabilities and speed, and limitations in internet connectivity. They also lack the advanced multimedia capabilities present in smartphones.

Since these devices don't support most of the Android applications available, you can prevent yourself from opening any shopping app on your device. The internet connectivity on these devices is also less advanced so that you can avoid most of the ad pop-ups.

If you feel you still need a smartphone, then you can install ad blockers on the device. This will prevent you from viewing ads, but you have to put in extra effort to avoid going to sites like Amazon or eBay.

You could write a whole book on this topic – in fact, I have. So much of our world is numbingly distracting, and my book on digital minimalism might help you if you're struggling, like many of us, when it comes to our devices.

Avoid Things or People That Promote Spending

Some friends lead you on spending sprees. Avoid them at all costs. These individuals may ruin your life without them realizing it.

If you enjoy their company, then make sure you meet them in places like parks or restaurants where you're less likely to overspend.

If you have things that trigger your spending, then do your best to avoid them. These can be the sight of a shopping mall, the smell of freshly baked bread, and so on.

Plan Your Day

Planning your day involves following a schedule. When you keep to this schedule, you can increase your productivity while limiting your chances of slipping into old habits.

When planning your day, you must include essential activities you want to engage in. These activities are crucial in occupying the time you previously spent engaging in old habits.

There are lots of activities you can engage in, and regardless of the activity you select, it won't work unless you create the right environment.

To do this, be sure you're engaging in these activities without any distractions around you. If you want to stop using your phone before bed, then move it out of the bedroom and place a book on your bedside table. You're more likely to pick up the first thing you see in any situation.

Developing Healthy Social Network Habits

Depending on how you use social media, you can stray away from the minimalist lifestyle. This lifestyle promotes the idea of building relationships with those around you.

When social networks start doing more harm than good, then it's time to take action. Deleting your social media apps isn't always the best way to fix this problem. You can start by unfriending and unfollowing people on these platforms.

On social networks, you follow some users for the content they provide and not because you know them. These are the users you need to eliminate from your list. If you have a massive fear of missing out (FOMO), then you need to ask yourself a series of questions.

- How much information can you realistically go through every day without it interfering with your life?
- Is this information helpful or just for entertainment?

The idea of unfollowing and unfriending is to help you become more selective. Those you choose to follow should be those that have a direct, positive impact on your life.

You should also remember to unsubscribe from blogs and social platforms. All blogs offer an opt-in form to get users to sign-up. Once you complete this form, you give the blog permission to keep you up-to-date with their newsletters.

How many of these newsletters do you read? These newsletters often fill your inbox and pile up as unread emails. Start unsubscribing today. You can cut down your subscription numbers from 50 blogs to just five essential blogs.

When you go through the process of unfollowing, unfriending, and unsubscribing, you find out that you get to cut down your screen time effectively. Now, what can you do with the extra time you create?

One thing you must remember is that social networks are a way to replace real-life interactions. Therefore, you need to start hanging out with your friends more and interact, just like the old days.

When I say interact, I mean you should have a real discussion. A major problem you can observe when eating out is that a lot of people gather at a table and keep tapping on their smartphones. No one is taking the time to interact.

If you want to improve the quality of your relationships while reducing smartphone usage, get everyone to put their phones aside when you're hanging out. You can make things fun by setting a rule that the first person to pick up their phone has to settle the bill.

What Are You Really Buying?

This is a huge question you must answer if you want to maintain your new spending habits. For different individuals, buying goes beyond the exchange of money for goods. It can be a complex in their life.

This is common with compulsive buyers. Through their purchases, they can experience feelings of confidence, or think that they are gaining admiration from their peers. Sometimes a compulsive buyer is just using those purchases to get an adrenaline rush, sometimes known as "retail therapy."

If you feel a compulsion to buy anything you think you don't need, then you must use this opportunity to evaluate yourself.

- What is it you really want to gain from this purchase?
- Why are you falling for this temptation?
- Is there a void you're trying to fill?

Taking time to deal with the issues discussed in this chapter will help you overcome temptation in your daily life. These also improve your chances of maintaining a clutter-free life.

The Takeaway

- Developing new habits is crucial in maintaining a clutter-free life. Your new habits should address your spending habits.
- Questioning your actions can help in protecting yourself from falling from temptations or traps to lure you to old habits.
- Learn to be content and find hobbies to distract you from old habits.
- Have a plan for each day, so there is no room for old habits to creep in.
- Develop healthy habits to address your social network usage.
- Learn about what you're buying. Is it the product, or a feeling?

AFTERWORD

Wow, you're here already? I am so glad you made it all the way. This is my greatest joy as a writer – thank you.

Throughout this book, I have extensively discussed the topic of decluttering. To achieve my goal of helping you deal with the clutter with your life, there were some essential concepts introduced. I know that some of this might be difficult, as decluttering our homes often means decluttering our hearts and minds. It's not as simple as it appears, and I make no judgment of you. We've all been there, and we're here to help each other.

Let's go back to the topic of "less is more." How can you apply this in your life? In what ways can you express the notion of minimalism in your everyday life, actions, words, emotions and in how you keep your home, car or office. These things sometimes seem unrelated, but really, they're not. Physical clutter is a symptom and one that requires deep work.

It's possible that you'll be able to quickly reorganize your bedroom, bathroom or kitchen, for example. But, as we go through our lives, looking at what we hang on to and why can be a completely freeing activity. By letting go of things, and keeping life simple, we free up our lives, and we can move more fluidly through our world.

How will you continue on your new minimalist journey? You've taken the first steps. Which direction will it lead you? Will you choose minimalism in how you see your place in the world by exploring eco-minimalism? Will you move down the pathway of material minimalism? Technology? A combination of them all?

Unstuff Your Home is so much more than this book title. As you literally declutter, you may have difficulties, even with family members who may not be on board.

With the knowledge you have now, the next step is to continue on your minimalist journey. There are different types of minimalists, including essential minimalists, eco-minimalists, and so on. Have you decided on the kind of minimalist lifestyle you want to adopt?

On this journey, having people to support will be beneficial. The first place where you must start is in your home. Is your family on board with the idea of minimalism? Are your friends going to be supportive? Even though you might feel alone in this process, always remember that I'm here, as a friend, and as a support.

To remain by your side on this journey, I have several other books you might also find helpful. These books focus on how you live a simpler and more satisfying life. Some of these I've mentioned before. You might find any of them helpful. Titles include:

- Minimalist
- Declutter
- Minimalist Living
- Digital Minimalism

If you're taking your first steps to declutter, just by reading this book, you've already come a long way. I wish you the best on your journey of decluttering your life!

REFERENCES

Aitchison, S. (2017). 5 Reasons Why Less Is More. Retrieved 18 January 2020, from https://www. stevenaitchison.co.uk/5-reasons-less/

Armstrong, L. (2020). Dangers of Hoarding and Cleanup Procedures | RestorationMaster Finder. Retrieved 18 January 2020, from https:// restorationmasterfinder.com/restoration/dangers-of-hoarding/

Avis-Riordan, K. (2018). Declutter: How to achieve a super-clean, organised & clutter-free bedroom. Retrieved 18 January 2020, from https:// www.housebeautiful.com/uk/lifestyle/storage/ a19562364/how-to-declutter-bedroom-storage-ideas/

Doland, E. (2010). Ask Unclutterer: Why do people struggle with clutter?. Retrieved 18 January

2020, from https://unclutterer.com/2010/09/17/ ask-unclutterer-why-do-people-struggle-with-clutter/

Jay, F. (2011). Minimalism Around the World: Danshari. Retrieved 18 January 2020, from http://www.missminimalist.com/2011/08/minimal-ism-around-the-world-Danshari/

Oppong, T. (2018). Wabi-Sabi: The Japanese Philosophy For a Perfectly Imperfect Life. Retrieved 22 January 2020, from https://medium.com/per-sonal-growth/Wabi-Sabi-the-japanese-philosophy-for-a-perfectly-imperfect-life-11563e833dc0

Palmer, B. (2013). How to Let Go of Inheritance and Gift Clutter. Retrieved 22 January 2020, from https://www.huffpost.com/entry/how-to-let-go-of-inherita_b_2903888?guccounter=1&guce_referrer= aHR0cHM6Ly93d3cuZ29vZ2xlLmNvbS8& guce_referrer_sig=AQAAAMXcvzOnSBYT_7zdCrj EF2RBeiea343usv_HNjCoNG2zWg4o4JdJZdwTz m1lQhbrvm9paFSkzJLgIvD4Cl8SjLJ5paBSd9IIba 97BZAKXSOYOCaETR2bHyw9IonOrkoNAzs5tu tw_Xl_wZRokZkcEuzSxTdleRpViuj9nnPlpdKX

Sewell, B. (2017). 6 eye-opening reasons why we accumulate clutter (and how to finally let go). Retrieved 18 January 2020, from https:// increasingselfworth.com/6-reasons-accumulate-clutter/

WANT TO LEARN MORE ABOUT MINIMALISM?

ALSO BY LILLY NOLAN

Minimalist: The Ultimate Guide to Organizing Your Home, Decluttering Your Mind, and Creating a Joyful Life

Would you like to wake up everyday in a cozy and beautiful home, surrounded ONLY by the objects that inspire you to live a meaningful life?

Would you like to live a simple life with absolutely NO clutter, stress, or anxiety?

Discover: The #1 secret to Significantly Improve Your Quality of Life

>> GET IT HERE:
http://www.amazon.com/dp/B07VJY39GZ

AUTHOR'S NOTE

Thank you so much for taking the time to read my book. I hope you have enjoyed reading this book as much as I've enjoyed writing it.

If you've enjoyed this book, please take a moment and write a short review. It will help me a lot and keep me going.

Thank you for supporting an individual author like me, this really means a lot!

Warm regards,

Lilly

ABOUT THE AUTHOR

Lilly Nolan is a Cleaning Coach and Minimalist who is on a mission to help people declutter their homes and ultimately simply their lives. Through strategic organization, she ensures a harmonious space is created that promotes joy instead of stress.

Before she discovered the art of minimalism, she was overwhelmed by the amount of housework she had to do. No matter how hard she tried, she felt like she was running behind. Thousands of minimalism articles and books later, she decided to put everything she learned into action and immediately felt an unshakable sense of freedom. Before she knew it, Lilly became a go-to tidying expert.

Printed in Great Britain
by Amazon